# A STRAIGHTFORWARD
# GUIDE TO
# THE RIGHTS OF THE CONSUMER

### DAVID BRYAN

STRAIGHTFORWARD PUBLISHING
WWW.STRAIGHTFORWARDCO.CO.UK

Straightforward Publishing
11 Lyndhurst Road
Hove
East Sussex

ISBN 1903909 37 6

Printed by CATS Solutions Wiltshire.

Cover design by Straightforward Graphics

Whilst every effort has been made to ensure that the information contained within this book is correct at the time of going to press, the author and publisher can take no responsibility for the errors or omissions contained within.

# A STRAIGHTFORWARD GUIDE TO THE RIGHTS OF THE CONSUMER

## CONTENTS

Introduction

# INTRODUCTION

This book has been written for the general public and also for the student of the law as it governs the consumer.

There are three legal systems in the United Kingdom: English Law, which covers Wales as well, Scottish law and Northern Irish law. In practice there is very little difference between English law and Northern Irish law so reference throughout this book will be to English law. Scottish law differs significantly. Courts have different procedures and some laws are different. There will be a brief resume of Scottish law in chapter 16.

The aim of the book is to outline the rights of the consumer when entering into a transaction with a seller of goods. Many people do not know their rights when encountering problems at the point of sale or after. What, for example, are your rights if goods turn out to be unsuitable or substandard and the seller refuses to let you have your money back or generally try's to tell you that there is nothing that can be done.

Another area which causes problems is that of consumer credit. Many people are taken in by what seem, on the face of it, to be favourable terms. However, the small print is rarely read and problems ensue. At the current time, the Government has put forward a White Paper which seeks to impose a greater regulatory framework on all areas of consumer credit as it is feared that individual borrowing is reaching unacceptable levels.

Hire agreements are also covered along with the sale of unsafe goods. Food safety and general hygiene are also outlined.

The rights of the consumer are quite considerable and yet most of us live in complete ignorance of exactly what they are. The obligations upon the shopkeeper and those who sell us goods generally are considerable, corresponding with consumer rights.

The primary purpose of this book is to educate the consumer and to empower him/her by fostering an understanding of the responsibilities of the seller. The responsibilities of the consumer in relation to transactions will also be pointed out.

It is hoped that all will benefit by reading this book. The rights of the consumer are of paramount importance and it is one area where general education leaves a lot to be desired.

# 1

# CONSUMER RIGHTS – AN OVERVIEW

All transactions between consumers and suppliers are based on the law of contract. Every exchange of goods is an agreement between buyer and seller.

It therefore follows that underlying each exchange is an area of law which defines the rights and obligations of both buyer and seller. The purchaser and the person who sells goods and services are not free to do exactly as they wish after the sale or, indeed, make up the rules as they go along.

*The major area of law which supports and assists consumers is the Sale of Goods Act 1979, as amended by the Sale and Supply of Goods Act 1994. This Act governs all transactions where goods are transferred for a price.*

There are, however, certain situations where a consumer will not be covered by the Sale of Goods Act. As was mentioned, this Act covers transactions where a sum of money is involved, where a price has been set for the goods. In some circumstances you may swap or exchange goods. In this case, the transaction will be governed by the Supply of Goods and Services Act 1982.

There are a number of transactions which may involve a combination of swap and cash, such as the trading-in of a product against a newer model. If an amount of cash is involved, no matter how small, then the Sale of Goods Act 1979 will apply.

## The contract of sale

There are what is known as "express and implied" conditions governing any contract, not just consumer contracts. Express terms of

9

the contract are those agreed by the buyer and seller. However, once it has been determined that the Sale of Goods Act covers the transaction there are certain conditions implied into the sale by the Act. These conditions cannot be circumvented by the seller.

*In every contract for the Sale of Goods, the 1979 Act states that where there is a sale of goods by description there is simultaneously an implied condition that the goods sold will match their description. In other words, the seller must sell you what has been described in the advertising. Nothing more and nothing less will suffice.*

Section 13 of the Sale of Goods Act applies to all sales, whether by private individuals or business. Anyone who sells a good to another is covered. Section 13 applies to all goods no matter what the purchasing situation. Just because, for example, the goods were on open display and the potential buyer can see what is on offer, does not mean that sale by description does not apply A tin of fruit might contain a different fruit to what is described in the tin or a sweater might in fact not be 100 per cent wool as it says on the label.

The golden rule which underpins the Act is that the description of the product on offer must match the product sold. As television shopping assumes greater prominence, in the form of television shopper channels, this Act will assume greater importance. No longer will there be the direct face-to-face contact between the buyer and the seller, only a telephone line. The process of challenging the product when you eventually receive it will be more long winded, as it often is with mail order of whatever description. However, consumers will need to be aware of their rights in the probable instance of receiving goods that do not correspond to what was requested. We will be discussing distance selling and the new Distance Selling Regulations 2000 further on in this book.

There may be cases where the consumer purchases goods and relies on a sample to make a choice. This is quite often the case when choosing fabric for furnishings or carpets. The Sale of Goods Act also covers samples and states that the goods must correspond with the description of those goods and not just the sample shown.

10

This is very important for those who feel let down by goods received by way of choosing from samples and wish to return those goods.

Remember THE SALE OF GOODS ACT 1979 SECTION 13 is the Act that you should refer to if you experience problems in this area.

*Your rights under this section entitle you to reject the goods and obtain a refund. It is not at the discretion of the seller, but your right.*

In addition to the goods not matching up to the description, section 30 of the Act also provides a remedy to the consumer if quantity of goods is not that which was requested or advertised. Quite simply, because a different amount is supplied then there has been a breach of description.

If the consumer receives a mixture of goods, for example, two saucepans ordered but the third different to the one described then the right exists to reject the goods. There is no right for the consumer to keep the goods. They must be returned if rejected.

Now read the key points from chapter 1.

# Key points from Chapter 1

- All consumer transactions are based on the law of contract. Every exchange of goods is an agreement between buyer and seller.

- The major area of law which supports and assists consumers is the Sale of Goods Act 1979 as amended by the Sale and Supply of Goods Act 1994.

- There are certain situations where the Sale of Goods Act will not apply. In this case the transaction is governed by the Supply of Goods and Services Act 1982.

- There are a number of transactions which may involve a combination of swap and cash. If an amount of cash is involved then the Sale of Goods Act 1979 will apply.

# 2

# DEFECTIVE GOODS

In the previous chapter we looked at consumer rights generally and pointed out the importance of the Sale of Goods Act 1979, as amended. In this chapter we will look at the area of law protecting consumers when a good or service supplied is defective.

We have all been in the situation where we have purchased something, and found it to be defective. In most cases, we can confidently assume that goods can be returned and exchanged or money refunded. However, this is not always the case and sometimes the seller will make life difficult, even going so far as to refuse to exchange goods or refund money.

This is a blatant breach of the law and of the rights of the consumer. Again, it is necessary to be able to quote the law and show that you mean business.

There are many examples of defective goods. This can range from the washing machine or fridge to the item of clothing that either has a defect or does not last the first wash.

*The Sale of Goods Act 1979 covers these situations. The seller has to be an established business however. It is most important to understand this point. The Act does not cover private sales. However, the purchaser can be business or private. There is no distinction here.*

Goods sold in the course of business must be what is known as "of merchantable quality'. Section 14 of the Sale of Goods Act defines this. Basically, goods are of a merchantable quality if they are as fit for the purpose for which goods of that kind are commonly bought. In other words, the good must be the same high quality as other goods of a similar kind. If they are not then they are defective.

The price of a good is of significant importance when considering the notion of merchantable quality. A product may be soiled in some way and not achieve the required standard. However, the actual cost of the good is of importance.

Sometimes you buy a good, find that it is defective, take it back and are told by the salesman that it can be repaired quite easily. What is your position then? The position is that you do not have to accept a repair to the item but can demand an exchange or refund. However, there will be cases where the repairing of an item is the only way forward from a practical point of view. This is quite reasonable in the circumstances.

Sometimes, and this is quite common, a guarantee will be given with a product. This gives the consumer an automatic right to a replacement if a good is defective. Guarantees and warranties are discussed further on in this book.

The situation is slightly different when the consumer purchases a second hand item. The same condition applies as to new good but obviously age and condition of the item have to be taken into account and the buyer should realise that there is a greater risk of a defect. However, the Sale of Goods Act still applies in the case of second hand goods.

There is however, one proviso here. That is that the Sale of Goods Act says that goods must be of merchantable quality unless the defect is pointed out to the buyer by the seller. Examination of the goods, and the acceptance of those goods provides a get out for many sellers.

This situation can be awkward as many buyers are keen to examine anything they buy. If you miss a defect in a good then the seller has the right to say that you should have noticed the defect. In many cases, of Course, the defect may not be readily apparent. If you do examine goods before purchase then it is highly advisable to check thoroughly before acceptance.

The Sale of Goods Act section 14 also governs what is known as "fitness of purpose". Fitness of purpose quite simply means that the goods purchased must be reasonably fit for the purpose for which they are made. For example, a purchase of a dishwashing machine would lead us to believe that we are buying something that can wash dishes. If this is not the case then the consumer has every right to return the goods.

There are examples here, though, where the buyer cannot demand recompense from the seller if he has not relied on the skill and judgement of the seller. A typical example may be where the buyer goes into a shop and demands something that he assumes is compatible with something else, for example, a printer which he asks for by name, receives it and subsequently finds that it is not fit for the purpose. The key is to ask as many questions as possible before purchasing in order to give the seller as much information as is needed to ensure that the good that he is selling is the correct good.

Buyers of goods have to understand the nature and consequences of *acceptance of goods*. The Sale of Goods Act sections 34 and 35 deal with acceptance. Section 35 is very important. Basically, if a buyer accepts goods then any damages payable on subsequently discovering a problem will be affected. Acceptance of a good or goods is recognised to occur in a number of ways. One such way is by intimation. This can occur when a buyer or business does not inspect goods, signs for them and only after discovers problems. There are acts after delivery which are not consistent with the sellers ownership. This is usually more important in commercial rather than straightforward consumer cases. If the buyer retains the goods beyond what is considered a reasonable time then this can constitute acceptance and can undermine the case for compensation.

It is true to say that most consumers would not look for damages if the good that they have purchased is defective in one way or another. Usually the act of replacing or repairing a good is seen as fair and equitable.

Now read the key points from Chapter 2.

# Key points from Chapter 2

- The Sale of Goods Act 1979 covers situations where goods are found to be defective.

- Goods sold in the course of business must be of 'merchantable quality'

- The price of a good is of importance when considering the notion of merchantable quality

- The Sale of Goods Act 1979 also covers 'fitness of purpose'. The goods purchased must be reasonably fit for the purpose for which they are intended

# 3

# OTHER TRANSACTIONS

In chapter two we looked at the law and defective goods, transactions between seller and buyer which are covered by the Sale of Goods Act. However, there are transactions which are not covered by the Act, simply because there is no "transfer of property for a monetary consideration called a price".

An example may be the purchase of a good under a hire purchase agreement. We will be discussing this in more depth later. However, purchase of goods in this way constitutes "bailment". In other words, the goods are owned by the hire purchase company until the last payment is made. If the good is defective in this case, what is the remedy? Hire purchase transactions of this kind are covered by the Supply of Goods (implied terms) Act 1973. Sections 9 and 10 are exactly the same as sections 13 and 14 of the Sale of Goods Act and therefore the remedy lies here.

There is another form of consumer transaction which needs to be understood. This is known as the *conditional sale transaction.* This is where a buyer of a good, a typical example being a car, may have the car for six months and have constant trouble. If the buyer experiences ongoing trouble and the garage is alerted then he will be entitled to a refund of his money.

There is an important point to be made here. That is the buyers attitude and whether or not he accepts the good even though it is defective. Two notions exist - acceptance and affirmation. What this means is that acceptance will occur when the buyer accepts delivery. However, affirmation can only occur when the defect is known, with time starting to run from that point. If the buyer simply carries on driving the car, or using the good even though there is knowledge of the defect then he is accepting the good and undermining his right to return or seek compensation. However, if the buyer does not affirm, i.e., continually lets the garage know that there has been problems, then he is not affirming the contract and will be entitled to a refund.

Be very careful here. Always assert your right, do not be afraid of complaining and keep a record of the number of times that you have complained.

### Use of materials when carrying out repairs

Responsibility, or liability, for parts under a contract which is for works and materials is regulated by sections 3 and 4 of part 1 of the Supply of Goods and Services Act 1973. If a remedy is needed for the supply of parts which are either defective or are not those which are supposed to have been used then it is to this Act that you must turn. As before, the notion of affirmation and acceptance is of paramount importance.

When it comes to the service element of a contract, as opposed to the materials element, then it is to section 13 of the Supply of Goods and Services that you must turn. Section 13 states that work must be carried out with reasonable care and skill.

There is one famous legal case which tends to set the standard in this area. This case was Bolam v Friern Hospital in 1957. This involved the medical profession and the issue was deciding whether a doctor is liable for negligence and comparisons with a so-called "average doctor". The connection here is that if you are complaining about standards of work then you would need to demonstrate that the average garage could have carried out the work to a higher standard.

There are other terms implied into a service contract. Section 14 implies that the business doing the servicing must carry it out within a reasonable time. This is where there are no express terms in the agreement. Section 15 indicates that where no price has been agreed then a reasonable price must be agreed. A reasonable price is one which another company would charge for the same work.

Therefore, if you feel that you are being overcharged then you can challenge it, underpinned by the backing of section 15 of this Act. There is one very important rider here. That is if the supplier has quoted a high price and the consumer has accepted then there can be no redress, not even if you find that another company will provide that service for far less.

CONSUMER BEWARE. Always shop around. If you feel that the price is too high then ask elsewhere. Always try to avoid entering into an agreement with no stated price.

Of course, there will always be the case where it is not really possible to get a price. This is where protection under section 15 comes in.

## EXAMPLE

*You discover that you are receiving electric shocks off your car. You telephone a local garage that specialises in car electric's and the owner tells you to "drop your car in". You do this and telephone the garage later to see what the problem is. The garage owner informs you that the problem was minor, with a power lead earthing. The problem has been rectified and you can collect the car. You do this and you are informed that the bill is £150. Quite rightly, you think that this is too high. Two things can happen here, and often do. On one hand the garage owner can tell you that that is what he charges and you must pay it. The other is that you can find out what an alternative garage would pay for the same work and establish a reasonable price, refusing to go above this.*

The problem that you have to sort out here is how to get your car back. You have to argue the case with the garage and let them know that you understand your rights as a consumer and you have read and understood the law that governs this particular problem.

It is the case that when businesses realise that they may get bad publicity and the person in front of them knows their rights, they generally back down, as it is bad for business. If there has been a breach of services contract then the normal solution or remedy is damages to put the defective or poor work right. Damages for distress or disappointment can be awarded in some cases although there are certain areas where it is difficult, such as holidays.

## The Consumer Protection Act 1987

The above Act covers those instances where a person has been injured because of a defective good. This Act also covers the many instances where someone may have been injured or affected who is not the principal purchaser but has been injured.

The Consumer Protection Act therefore imposes a very strict liability for defective goods on someone who is deemed to be the producer of the product. The Act provides, or at least seeks to provide, a route for the consumer to seek redress against the person who is ultimately responsible for the damage. This gets rid, or at least minimises the requirement to have to prove fault, which in the past has proven very time consuming and difficult and also very expensive.

The Act is only relevant where the consumer has purchased a defective product which has caused damage. It is essential to determine who is liable, and the Act says that the following are primarily liable for damages:

a) the producer

b) an own brander who has held himself to be the producer of a particular good

c) the first importer into the European Community. Therefore, strict liability will attach to any person or company who presents its/his self as producer of a good.

Only in a few cases will the supplier of a good be liable. These cases are limited to instances where it may not be possible to identify the producer or anyone else within or further up the chain, in a reasonable period of time.

It is necessary to define product. This is because some goods and services are more readily identifiable than others as products. Section 1(2) of the Act defines product and has wide definitions. For example, goods include electricity. Section 45 also defines goods produced from the land, such as crops, and other goods such as aircraft vehicles etc. A product, however, is a common sense notion and for the purposes of the every day consumer a product is fairly obvious.

A defective product is simply where the safety of the product is in question and can be a manufacturing defect, a design defect and a defect that has arisen because of a misleading warning notice. In this latter instance, this means a notice that has failed to advise the consumer how to use a product properly.

A consumer can sue under the Consumer Protection Act (s5) for:

- Death caused as a result of a defective product

- Personal injury caused as a result of a defective product

- Damage to private property, above a certain sum, caused as a result of a defective product.

The is no liability for any damage to the product itself or for the loss of, or any damage to, the whole or any part of any product which has been supplied with a product.

There are cases where, even if a manufacturer is liable under the Act, the Act contains what is known as strict liability and not absolute liability. This means that there are a number of defences that can be used by manufacturers. It is up to the defendant, i.e., the manufacturer to prove one of the following as a defence:

- The defect was caused by the need to comply with the law as it stands at that time. This may have been the need to comply with new legislation that has recently been introduced

- The manufacturer did not supply the product in question-this can relate to instances of theft

- That the supplier of the good is not in business and is a private individual. Remember, the aim of the Act is to impose strict liability on commercial producers and it is not really the intention, or the spirit of the Act to impose any liability on individuals as such. However, individuals who are not in business are not ruled out.

- That the defect did not exist in the product at the time of supply. One very good example has been the recent spate of contaminating certain products as they lay on shelves, such a baby food and also chocolate. If contamination takes place in the shop then it is important to note that the seller, or retailer becomes liable under the Sale of Goods Act.

Another defence, perhaps the most complicated and controversial is that of the state of scientific (and technical) knowledge at the time was not such that a producer of products of the same description as the product in question might be expected to have discovered. Here, a producer of a product has to demonstrate that at the time in question they could not be expected to know of the defect:

Finally, that the producer of a component part of a product had produced a defective product and the defect was as a result of instructions given by the main producer.

A consumer may bring a claim against a manufacturer within a certain timescale - in relation to personal injuries or any damage to property there is a three year time period within which to bring a claim. However, as far as a manufacturer of a product is concerned, there is a 10-year cut off point from the time that a particular product was supplied to a retailer.

There are some instances where a recall notice may be issued by a manufacturer to a retailer. This is happening all the time, in the cases of bay food, cars and other items. This in no way relieves the manufacturer of liability although it can certainly help to reduce the amount of compensation gained by an aggrieved person.

Now read the key points from Chapter 3.

## Key points from Chapter 3

- The Sales of Goods Act does not cover situations where there has been a transfer of property at no price

- An example may be a purchase of a good under a hire purchase agreement

- Hire purchase transactions of this kind are covered by the Supply of Goods and Services Act (implied terms) 1973

- There is another form of consumer transaction called the conditional sale transaction. This is where the buyer of a good experiences trouble and will be entitled to his money back

- Responsibility for works and materials under a contract is governed by the Goods and Services Act 1973

- The Consumer Protection Act 1987 covers consumers who have been issued because of a defective good

# 4

# GUARANTEES AND WARRANTIES

In the previous chapter we looked at defective goods and consumer remedies. In this chapter we will concentrate on the situation concerning guarantees and warranties issued by manufacturers.

A guarantee is most often issued by the manufacture of goods such as electrical goods, or by a company providing services such as replacement windows. It is normally provided free of charge when you buy the good or service. A guarantee usually offers to carry out repairs or make a replacement in the event of a fault arising.

## Warranties

A warranty provides the same sort of cover that a guarantee does, but often you have to pay extra for it – for example many electrical stores provide warranties for five years, at a cost. These sort of warranties are, effectively, insurance policies.

## Legal protection with guarantees and warranties

Because guarantees are provided free by manufacturers, the law considers most guarantees to be merely a promise. Unless you bought the goods directly from the manufacturer you will have no claim against them However, most manufacturers will honour guarantees as to not do so would lead to them having a bad name.

The situation is different with a warranty. This is because you will have usually paid for it. This will then change the status of a warranty from a mere promise to do something, into a contractual obligation, which is enforceable in law. If a company does not honour a warranty then they can be sued.

## Frequent problems

*Fridge freezer purchased 13 months ago and the fridge section has completely failed.*

When you buy goods from a shop, you enter into a contract under the Sale of Goods Act 1979 which holds the shop liable for up to six years after purchase, providing that you can demonstrate that the problem is down to an unreasonable fault and not wear and tear. The guarantee issue is not relevant here. That is merely a promise by the manufacturer.

*Damp proofing course carried out 5 years ago by a limited company, but noticed rising damp once again. Company claims that it was taken over by new owners and refuses to honour the original 10-year guarantee.*

Your contract was with the original company and you cannot enforce the contract or any guarantees. Insurance does exist new for this type of problem

Read any guarantees or warranties carefully – get them in writing!

Now read the key points from Chapter 4

Key points from Chapter 4

- A guarantee is most often issued by manufacturers of goods and will offer to carry out repairs or replace parts in the event of a fault

- A warranty provides the same sort of cover that a guarantee does, but often the consumer will have to pay extra for it

- Always read guarantees and warranties carefully

# 5

# ATTEMPTS TO DENY LIABILITY FOR A PRODUCT

In the last chapter, we looked at guarantees and warranties and the rights and obligations of the consumer. In this chapter we will look at attempts to exclude or deny liability for a product.

We have all seen notices on products which say that the manufacturer is excluded from all liability for a good. This is a very important area and we need to look at the actual liability of a manufacturer even if an exclusion notice has been given. There is nothing stopping a shopkeeper or manufacturer from stonewalling your claim for damages due to the fact that an exclusion notice has been attached to a product.

Typical exclusion notices might read:

"No responsibility will be accepted for goods once they have left the store"
"There will be no refund for this good, even if found to be unsuitable"
"We accept no returns under any circumstances"

The list is endless and can apply to a whole range of products. However, what the consumer needs to know is whether a retailer can actually impose any of these restrictions. Can a retailer avoid the liabilities imposed under the Sale of Goods Act or the Supply of Goods Act or any other Act?

There is one major starting point for all exclusion notices. What we need to determine is whether or not the notice has been incorporated, or is an integral part of, the contract for sale. If this has not occurred then there can be no exclusion notice. Incorporation means that if a consumer signs a contract they are bound by it, in the absence of any sort of misrepresentation. So, if a consumer has signed a contract they are bound by its terms. However, if the terms contained in an unsigned document which is an exclusion notice, the terms will only form part of the actual contract if there has been an attempt to bring the notice to the consumers attention.

The Unfair Contract Terms Act 1977 is of importance in determining whether or not a consumer has signed an unfair, or onerous contract. The Act will govern any clause which purports or attempts to restrict liability. The Act governs business and will control the acts of a person who, through contract, attempts to deny any liability for a good where, in fact, there does exist a liability in law.

If we look at the matter objectively, as we have seen so far there are a range of laws which protect the consumer and place obligations on manufacturers and suppliers. Merely to insert an exclusion clause, thereby giving full protection against the law, is an absurdity.

In practice, the unfair Contract Terms Act operates in three areas:

- Where there are exclusions in relation to the implied terms section of the Sale of Goods Act 1979 and the 1982 Sale of Goods Act (implied Terms).

- The person supplying the goods is trying to avoid negligence based liability;

- The person supplying the goods is trying to avoid liability for any other breach of contract.

*Example A removal firm undertakes to do a job for Mr and Mrs Smith. They inform the couple that their liability for any damages to goods is covered by an exclusion clause in a contract that they wish to sign. This states that liability for any damage is limited to £35 per item or £100 in total.*

Can they do this? What they are trying to do is to avoid the above Acts which impose liabilities for negligence and the answer would be no, they cannot limit there own liability.

A very important point to note is that if you are dealing with a retailer as a consumer then the retailer cannot avoid responsibility as contained in the implied terms of contract which are governed by the Sale of Goods and Supply of Goods Acts.

There may be occasions where other goods, such as exchanged goods, hire goods or the materials part of a contract are concerned and the Supply of Goods Act (implied terms) and Sale of Goods Act do not apply. The Supply of Goods and Services Act governs these areas and section seven of the Unfair Contract Terms Act refers.

The Unfair Contract Terms Act also covers negligence based clauses, i.e., where a manufacturer denies liability for negligence. Section 1 of the UCTA defines negligence as the breach of duty of care arising in contract.

As far as the consumer is concerned, the area which is most likely to arise is an attempt to avoid liability for a breach of section 13 of the Supply of Goods and Services Act.

Section 2 of the Unfair Contract Terms Act says that any clause (or notice) is invalid insofar as it attempts to exclude liability for negligence *resulting in death or personal injury.*

Section 2(2) of the Act also goes on to state that if any other loss or damage arises as a result then the clause of the notice will only be valid provided a reasonableness test is satisfied.

The reasonableness test contains guidelines and include:

a) the strength of the bargaining position between parties to a contract
b) whether there was any inducement to agree to the term, i.e., was there any special offer or was the consumer put in a position where he/she had to agree before purchase;
c) whether the consumer knew of any term in the first place;
d) whether the goods were specially manufactured.

The Unfair Contract Terms Act also deals with other breaches of contract such as where a business will try to exclude or restrict liability to a certain sum or claims to be entitled to give a good or service which is in fact substantially different to that stated. A common example here is that of a tour operator stating that they have the right to offer alternative holidays. The UCTA also covers the notice which claims to have no liability for the non delivery of a service.

Section 4 of the Act states that a person dealing as a consumer cannot be made to indemnify another person against liability for negligence or breach of contract unless the reasonableness test has been passed. Section 5 deals with manufacturers guarantees to the consumer and states that if goods which are supplied for private use or consumption prove defective whilst in use and cause loss or damage as a result of negligence in manufacture or distribution, then any attempt to avoid liability in a guarantee is void.

If misrepresentation is involved, then any attempt to exclude liability for misrepresentation is only valid provided that the reasonableness test is passed.

There are areas of law which will make it a criminal liability to give an exclusion notice. The Consumer Transactions (Restrictions on Statements) Order 1976 as amended, makes it a criminal offence to use a void exemption clause in a contract. Therefore, a notice such as no refunds etc., can make the seller criminally liable. The order also makes it an offence to supply goods to a consumer with written exclusion notices without pointing out that a consumers statutory rights are unaffected.

**The effect of the European Community and European Directives.**
There are attempts to make liability for consumer goods standard throughout the European Community and there is a European Directive on unfair terms in Consumer contracts which will seek to give the consumer more power, particularly when dealing with large companies or corporations. Contracts which operate to the detriment of the consumer will not be allowed. The draft directive is concerned only with contracts between business and consumers. No contracts will be excluded from the directive.

Now read the Key points from Chapter 5

# Key points from Chapter 5

- There is one major starting point for all exclusion notices – this is whether the notice has been incorporated into the contract for sale. If not the notice has no validity

- If there is an exclusion notice within a contract the Unfair Contract Terms Act 1997 will determine whether or not the contract is onerous

- The Unfair Contract Terms Act also covers negligence clauses in contracts

- There are areas of law that make it a criminal offence to provide exclusions in contracts

# 6

# BUYING GOODS AT HOME

In the previous chapter, we looked at consumer rights when a manufacturer attempts to deny or to exclude liability. In this chapter we will look at consumer rights when buying goods at home, in particular we will look at The Distance selling Regulations 2000.

Many people buy goods using the internet or fax, or from home shopping on the TV, or from catalogues. The law recognises that this type of shopping comes with its own type of problems. For example, what happens if the goods do not turn up or you don't like them once you have received them? People who shop at home now have rights under the Consumer Protection (Distance Selling) Regulations 2000.

Briefly, these Regulations say that you should be given clear information about the order and the company, along with a cooling off period, and protection against credit card fraud and the menace of unsolicited goods.

What isn't covered by these regulations?
- Financial services like banking and insurance
- Auctions
- Goods bought from a vending machine
- Goods bought using a payphone
- Contracts for the sale of land
- Food and drink, or other goods for everyday consumption delivered by rounds men

- Accommodation, transport, catering and leisure facilities for a specific time or date
- Timeshare and package holidays
- The regulations only apply when you buy from a trader who is organised to sell to you without face-to-face contact. So, if you saw something in a shop, went home and bought by phone, this is not distance selling.

## The right to clear information

Before you decide to buy, the seller must give you the following information:

- The name of the trader, along with their postal address if you have to pay in advance
- An accurate description of the goods and services
- The price, along with any taxes or delivery charges if relevant and how long the price or offer remains valid
- Delivery arrangements, which should be within 30 days unless agreed otherwise
- Payment arrangements
- The right to cancel the order .
- Information about whether you will be liable for the cost of returning the goods if you change your mind
- For services provided over a period of time, such as a mobile phone contract, or a gas supply contract, you must be told what the duration of that contract will be

After you buy, the trader must provide you with the following information:

- Written confirmation of your order (by letter, e-mail or fax) including the information outlined above, if not already provided
- Written information on how to cancel, a contact postal address and details of any guarantees, warranties or after sales service
- Details of how and when to end a contract for the provision of a service if there is no specified finish date
- This information should be sent to you by the time the goods are delivered.

## Your right to cancel

The Distance Selling Regulations 2000 give you the right to change your mind and cancel an order within seven working days. If you do decide to cancel, then you should put this in writing, either by letter or you can fax or e-mail. The time limits are:

- For goods – seven working days after the day on which the goods are received

- For services – seven working days after the day on which you agreed to go ahead with the agreement

*What isn't covered by this cooling off period?*
- Services that are to be provided within seven working days. If you have agreed that the service will be provided before the end of the cooling off period you will not be entitled to cancel once the service has started, but the trader must tell you this in writing.

- Goods made to your personal requirements or specifications

- Goods which may deteriorate quickly, such as flowers or food

- Sealed audio or video recordings or computer software that have been opened.

- Betting, gaming or lottery services

- Newspapers, periodicals or magazines.

Now read the Key points from Chapter 6

Key points from Chapter 6

- The rights of consumers who purchase goods over the internet, television or some other distance selling outlet are covered by the Consumer protection (Distance Selling) Regulations 2000

- There are a number of items not covered by the above regulations

- There is a right to clear information from distance selling traders

- There is a clear right to cancel a purchase

# 7

# CONSUMERS AND DIFFERENT TYPES OF CREDIT

In the previous chapter we looked at the law concerning buying goods at home, in particular the Distance Selling Regulations 2000, which have greatly strengthened consumer rights. In this chapter we will look at the all important area of consumer credit.

At the time of writing, 2004, the Government has introduced a White Paper which seeks to tighten up on the laws governing consumer credit, specifically the area of credit cards, which they see as out of control. Leading to unacceptable levels of consumer debt. For more details on this you should contact one of the consumer organisations listed in the back of this book.

The most important Act dealing with consumers and credit is the Consumer Credit Act 1974.

The aims of the 1974 Act are:

a) to regulate the formation, terms and enforcement of credit and hire agreements. The Act gives consumers many rights and places restraints upon the enforcement of an agreement against a consumer.

b) the Act sets up a licensing system whereby those engaged in any form of consumer credit business must be licensed.

c) the true cost of credit must be shown plus the annual rate of interest.

It also controls door-to-door canvassing for credit. There are a number of common types of credit agreements-hire purchase is one such credit arrangement.

Hire purchase, as mentioned, is the bailment of goods with the option to purchase. The consumer (debtor) purchases a good, but does not, or cannot, afford to buy outright. The actual financing is done via a finance company. Whilst all negotiations and agreements are usually done with the business directly selling you the good, it is the finance company who will own the good. The finance company bails out the good to the consumer with the option to purchase. The debtor is actually contracting with the finance company and not the seller for the purchase of the good.

If the good turns out to be defective then the consumer's rights under the Sale of Goods Act are exercisable against the finance company.

There is an agreement known as the conditional sale agreement. This is a sale of goods subject to a condition and the condition is that the property will not pass until the goods have been paid for. As in hire purchase the finance company has legal title to the goods until the last instalment is paid.

The conditional sale agreement works in the same way as a hire purchase agreement The only difference is that the transaction is governed by the Sale of Goods Act 1979 and not the Supply of Goods (implied terms) Act 1973.

There is a form of agreement known as a credit sale agreement. This situation usually occurs when a store is financing its own goods to increase sales. Under this type of agreement the goods pass to the consumer straight away as opposed to a finance company. The transaction is covered by the Sale of Goods Act If services are being purchased then the transaction will be covered by the Supply of Goods and Services Act 1982.

## Using a credit card

When the consumer uses a credit card to finance a purchase, as is often the case today, then the buyer is entering into a contract with the store to supply the goods. The consumer agrees to pay the card off and the store will obtain refund less commission from the card company.

Quite often, credit card companies will offer their own guarantee when purchasing goods and it is very important to make sure that you understand what the card company is offering.

## Obtaining a loan where the loan company is connected to the supplier

In this situation, the debtor agrees to purchase goods or services from a supplier. The supplier has an arrangement with a finance company where the finance company agrees to loan all the suppliers clients money to purchase a good. The arrangement is then between the finance company and the supplier. The contract of sale and subsequent disputes between the buyer and seller are direct and governed by the Sale of Goods Act 1979.

One other situation is where the buyer obtains a personal loan to purchase a good, there is no link between the loan and the seller, in this case. The contract for the loan is between the buyer and loan-company and the contract for sale is between the buyer and seller.

The examples listed above are the most common examples of consumer credit.

In order to fully understand the workings of the Consumer Credit Act we need to look at definitions of credit contained within the Act.

The definitions of credit are contained within sections 8-20 of the Act. Most of the controls and restrictions in the Act apply only to what is known as "regulated Agreements" For an agreement to be regulated it must fall within the definition of a consumer credit agreement contained in section 8 of the Act The agreement is a regulated one under section 8 as long as it is not exempted under section 16. So, in order to find out if your agreement is regulated, you have to ascertain whether or not it is exempt. If it is not exempt, it is regulated.

Section 8 sets out monetary limits. This section states that an agreement by which the creditor provides the individual (the word individual also encompasses partnerships, but not companies) with credit not exceeding £15,000 (this is changed from time to time) is regulated. This is therefore the first factor which must be considered when determining whether an agreement is regulated. Many lenders, because of this amount, will only lend above £15,000 in order not to be caught by the Act.

Very often, agreements will have a total repayment well in excess of £15,000 when all charges are taken into account. However, the significant figure for determining is the fixed sum credit. This means that it is the amount lent not the final figure payable Where the credit is what is known as "running account", meaning that the debtor has been given a pre-set credit limit by the creditor, the significant figure is the credit limit.

Running account and fixed sum credit are defined by section 109 of the Act. Section 10(3) provides a little more protection for the person with the running account credit by saying that they are protected by the act if the amount that they can withdraw is less than £15,000 at a time.

The next important definition of a regulated agreement is that the agreement must either be restricted use credit or unrestricted use credit. If the debtors use to which he/she can put the credit is in some way restricted by the creditor, then the credit is restricted use.

*Example*

*A finance company will only lend the money if a certain item or items are purchased with it. The lender is not free to take the cash.*

46

When a purchaser uses a credit card to buy goods, then that card is restricted to that store or other stores which might take the card. This is therefore restricted credit.

The next, and perhaps the most significant definition of whether or not a contract is regulated is that of whether the agreement is a debtor-creditor-supplier agreement or a debtor-creditor agreement. Generally speaking, the debtor achieves a much higher level of protection if his credit agreement can be classed as a debtor-creditor-supplier agreement.

Under the Consumer Credit Act, the word "supplier" means the person the debtor has legally contracted to obtain the goods or services from, not the person who actually hands them over. One example here is where the buyer obtains the goods on hire purchase and the finance company has bailed them out to him. The finance company is the supplier not the shop with whom the purchaser has been dealing.

On the basis of the above definitions, it can be seen that all credit agreements need to be categorised into:

a) price limits

b) fixed sum or running account credit

c) restricted use or unrestricted use credit

d) Debtor-creditor or debtor-creditor-supplier agreements

e) two or three party debtor-creditor-supplier agreements.

We need to look at agreements which are exempt under section 16 of the Consumer Credit Act. It is important that you understand these definitions, particularly if you are going to challenge an agreement.

47

The first four exemptions relate to land mortgages. Most first land mortgages are outside of the Act. A number of second mortgages not used to finance the purchase of land will fall into the Act.

Debtor-creditor-supplier agreements for running account credit where the debtor has to repay the balance in a single payment. These agreements are exempt from the Act. This is usually of most relevance where you have purchased a good using a card like American Express.

Debtor-creditor agreements where the cost of credit is very low are exempt. Very low is defined as meaning where the annual rate does not exceed 13% or 1% above the highest of any base rates published by the English and Scottish clearing banks.

Every other agreement where the sum loaned is less than £15,000 is a regulated agreement.

What the consumer will wish to know is: how can he/she get out of a credit agreement as cheaply as possible. Before we examine this question in more depth we should look a little closer at the licensing system.

The Consumer Credit Act 1974 established a licensing system in an attempt to regulate the credit industry. This involves a system whereby licences can be issued to groups or individuals. Licences last for five years. An application for a licence can be refused or a licence can be suspended. Licences are required by: .

a) anyone who lends money not in excess of £15,000 to individuals;

b) anyone who passes an individual on to a source of finance (a credit broker);

c) anyone who operates a credit reference agency;

d) anyone who gives consumer debt advice.

The penalties for operating without a licence are both civil and criminal. In relation to civil sanctions, if a lender attempts to enforce an agreement and that person has not got a licence then the agreement is unenforceable. It is always worth checking that the person has a licence, or company has a licence.. In addition, if the credit broker is unlicensed but the creditor was licensed, once again the agreement is unenforceable without a validating order.

Whenever a debtor wishes to escape an agreement then a check should always be made as to whether the broker is licensed. There is a register of licensed brokers kept in London.

The Consumer Credit Act also controls agreements. The Act sets out the form that agreements should take. In addition, the Act also regulates the look of the agreement, such as colour and size of print etc. in order to ensure that it is understood by the person signing it.

If the creditor fails to comply with the formalities, the agreement is said to be improperly executed. In this case, the agreement cannot be enforced against the debtor without a court order.

Sections 60 and 61 of the Act enable regulations to be made to ensure that the debtor is aware of his/her obligations and rights. In particular, credit agreements should make clear the amount and timing of repayments, the Annual Percentage rate (APR) and the protection and remedies available to the debtor under the Act. The Act also sets out how many copies of the agreement the debtor should have.

The initial stages of a credit agreement, when a person completes the forms detailing income etc. amount to an *unexecuted agreement*. In this situation, the purchaser must be given a copy of what it is he/she has signed. When the deal is accepted by the finance company, a copy of the executed agreement must be sent to the debtor.

If instant credit is offered and everything is done on the spot, then the agreement is executed and offered and the debtor will have one copy at the outset.

Therefore, when the agreement is unexecuted the debtor receives two copies of the agreement, one at the outset and one on final execution. If the agreement is executed at the outset then the debtor will receive one copy.

In the case of a cancellable agreement changes are made to the provisions covering copies:

Now read the Key points from Chapter 7.

## Key points from Chapter 7

- The most important Act dealing with consumers and credit is the Consumer Credit Act 1974.

- The aims of the 1974 Act are to regulate the formation terms and enforcement of credit and hire agreements

- The Act sets up a licensing system whereby those engaged in any form of consumer credit business must be licensed.

- The conditional sale agreement is central to the 1974 Act.

- Quite often credit card companies will offer their own guarantee when purchasing goods and it is very important to make sure that you understand what the card company is offering.

# 8

# WITHDRAWAL FROM AN AGREEMENT

In the previous chapter we looked at consumers and credit. This is one of the most complex areas one can enter into and it is very important that you have a firm understanding. In this chapter, we will look at what happens when the consumer wants to withdraw from an agreement.

One of the cheapest ways of escaping from an agreement is to argue that there is no agreement in existence between the seller and buyer, that offer and acceptance has not occurred. This relates to the receipt if an unexecuted and executed agreement.

The final cheap way of escaping from an agreement is that of cancellation. The first step is to determine whether or not it is cancellable. Normally, where offer and acceptance has occurred, the agreement is binding on both parties. However, there is one escape route provided by Section 67 of the Consumer Credit Act.

By section 67, where oral representations have taken place in antecedent negotiations in the debtors presence and the agreement has been signed away from the trade premises of the creditor, the negotiator (i.e. the supplier or credit broker) or a party to a linked transaction, then the agreement is cancellable. Thus, if the buyer is allowed to take the agreement home and sign it then the agreement is cancellable.

Antecedent negotiations as defined by section 56 of the Consumer Credit Act includes anything said about the goods or credit by the creditor or the credit broker or the supplier in the debtors presence. Telephone negotiations are not covered as it is easy for the debtor to merely put the phone down.

## Cancellation or cooling off period

As has been discussed, if the agreement was unexecuted the buyer should receive through the post within seven days the executed copy. Both the first and second copy should contain notice of cancellation rights. If the agreement was executed at the outset then a second notice of cancellation rights should be sent by post within seven days.

It is the receipt of the second copy or notice that begins the cooling off period. This period is five days following the day the second copy or notice is received.

The aim of cancellation is to restore the parties to the position they would have been in had the agreement never been concluded. Goods are returned and money handed back.

If there is a part exchange involved, particularly where motor vehicles are concerned, then under section 73, once the debtor has cancelled the agreement, the negotiator (credit broker or supplier) must hand back the part exchange car or its monetary value within 10 days.

Now read the Key points from Chapter 8.

## Key points from Chapter 8

- One of the cheapest ways of escaping from an agreement is to argue that there is no agreement in existence

- The other way of escaping from an agreement is that of cancellation, if the agreement is cancellable

- There is one escape route provided by s 67 of the Consumer credit Act – this is where a buyer has been allowed to take an agreement home and sign it

# 9

# DEFECTIVE GOODS PURCHASED ON CREDIT

In the previous chapter, we looked at the position of the consumer when wishing to withdraw from an agreement. In this chapter we will look at the position of the consumer when purchasing goods on credit.

The consumers recourse to change of goods or money back will lie with whomever he/she has the agreement. We have seen that the business with whom the purchaser has the contract will be liable under the various Acts for defective goods.

### Unable to meet repayments

The first action here should be for the consumer to try to reach an agreement with the creditor. The creditor, when making a decision will be influenced by a number of factors, such as the saleability of the goods.

The type of credit agreement must be considered here. If the agreement is a loan the main principle is that it must be repaid. The only escape route, or breathing space for the debtor is that time to repay may be given.

If the agreement is a hire purchase or conditional sale agreement, then the finance company has legal title to the goods and one of the options open to the debtor who does not wish to keep the goods is to exercise his rights to terminate under section 99-100 of the Consumer Credit Act. This is a costly option. For termination to operate under section 99:

a) the agreement must be regulated under the Consumer Protection Act;

b) it is available at any time before the final payment becomes due;

c) all arrears must be paid;

d) the debtor is liable to pay the creditor half of the total price.

All of the above examples have been based on the fact that the consumer may wish to keep the goods. There may be a situation where the debtor might want to hang on to the goods. This also depends on the type of the credit agreement. If the agreement is a loan then it must be repaid. The goods purchased are the debtors and can be sold to repay the loan. If a debtor gets into any kind of financial difficulties then a default notice will be served on him by the finance company. This notice must be served before any further action can be taken. At least seven days must be given to remedy the breach. The debtor, in response can, if he wishes apply to the court for a time order This gives more time to pay off arrears.

The debtor can also retain goods by making them "protected". This means, basically, that he finance company, or whoever owns the goods will have to obtain a court order before the goods can be seized. This take time and the debtor will gain longer to pay off debts owed.

The Consumer Credit act also provides that goods are protected if the debtor has paid more than one third of the total price, the debtor is in breach of the agreement, the agreement is still valid and the property is owned by the creditor. If the creditor does seize the goods back without a court order, the agreement is terminated and the debtor can obtain all money paid to date as a refund.

## The Consumer Credit Act and "Extortionate credit bargains"

This is a fairly new concept, having been introduced into the Consumer Credit Act in 1978. The extortionate credit bargains provisions apply even if the credit exceeds £15,000. The Act (s138) states that a bargain is extortionate if it requires the debtor to make payments which are grossly exorbitant. The concept of grossly exorbitant will take into account interest rates prevailing at the time of the transaction and also other factors such as the relationship of the creditor with the debtor. The debtor can take proceedings through the county court to have the bargain re-examined and reopened.

## The position when purchasing hire goods

There has been a marked increase in the incidence of hired goods during the last ten years. This is partly to do with the cyclical nature of our economy and the fact that it is quite often cheaper to hire goods than to buy them. In addition, if a person needs an expensive good, such as a floor sander, for a few days only then it is obviously cheaper to rent than buy.

The Sale of Goods Act does not cover hired items as there has been no transfer of goods. However, Part 1 of the 1982 Supply of Goods Act covers hired goods. Exclusion notices are covered by the Unfair Contract Terms Act, section 7

Section 101 0f the Supply of Goods Act 1982 governs the right of the hirer to terminate the agreement after 18 months, even if the hire period was longer. All money due within the 18 months must be paid

Now read the Key points from Chapter 9.

## Key points from Chapter 9

- The consumers recourse to change of goods or money back will lie with whomever he or she had the agreement with, i.e. the trader

- The first action is for the buyer to try to reach an agreement with the seller

- The type of credit agreement signed will influence the trader and also affect the rights of the buyer

# 10

# THE TRADE DESCRIPTIONS ACT

In the previous chapter we looked at defective goods purchased on credit and the rights of the consumer. In this chapter, we will look at the Trade Descriptions Act and the rights of the consumer.

We have all seen goods that are described in weird and wonderful ways and yet, when we actually examine the good it is nothing special and does not match up to what we were led to believe.

The 1968 Trade Descriptions Act regulates the way business can describe their products. Section 1(1) states that any person who, in the course of a trade or business:

a) applies a false trade description to any goods; or
b) supplies or offers to supply any goods to which a false trade description is applied shall be guilty of an offence.

Section 2 of the Act lists 10 ways in which a trade description can be applied. These cover most eventualities. The most common offences are related to the motor industry, in particular to second hand cars and the falsifying of mileage.

Breach of the Trade Descriptions Act is a criminal offence. The maximum fine is usually no higher than £5,000. However, persistent breach of trade description, with a direct attempt to falsify, can lead to imprisonment.

Breach of the Trade Descriptions Act is only committed by someone in the course of business. Private individuals are not usually covered by the Act. Some traders will try to avoid liability by disclaiming-i.e., issuing a disclaimer notice. The issuing of disclaimers is subject to many restrictions. In order to be effective the disclaimer must have been issued before the trader supplied the goods. Sentences in small print are ineffective and general notices are also redundant.

Even if a trader complies with the above then if it is seen that the issue of a disclaimer is an attempt to avoid liability, in the full knowledge that a good is, or may be, defective, then a trader will still be liable.

Counterfeit goods have caused problems, particularly in recent years. There are other Acts, such as The Trade Marks Act 1938 or The Copyright Designs and Patents Act 1988 which can prevent traders from passing off imitations as the real thing. Typical imitations are substituting imitation Levi's or watches.

If, however, you are sold a product and receive no notice that it is not the real thing, then subsequently discover that it is an imitation, then you can sue under the Trade Descriptions Act.

The supply of services is covered by section 14 of the Trade Descriptions Act. Section 14 states that:

'It shall be an offence for any person in the course of trade or business to make a statement which he knows to be false or recklessly to make a statement which is false as to services, accommodation or facilities'.

This has been particularly relevant to holidays in recent years. Holiday companies make all sorts of promises and when the unsuspecting holidaymaker arrives abroad, they are often horrified to discover that the hotel is completely lacking in facilities claimed and their holidays are ruined.

Section 14 of the Act, as we have seen states that it is an offence for the person in the course of trade to "knowingly" or "Recklessly" make a statement which is false. Therefore, it is necessary to prove that what was said was a deliberate lie, or was said recklessly and, even though not intended to deceive, led to a breach of the Trade Descriptions Act.

Holiday companies are now also regulated by a European Directive, the Package Travel package Holidays and Package Tours Regulations 1992. These regulations create a civil and criminal liability and apply to all packages sold in the United Kingdom after December 31st 1992. The regulations create strict guidelines and have closed many loopholes. The Regulations cover price, accommodation, information. Liability for damages is also defined more clearly. The Department of Trade and Industry have a leaflet available which expands on the obligations of the tour industry.

## Defences to a Trade Descriptions Claim

Section 24 of the Trade Descriptions Act states that it shall be a defence for the person charged to prove that:

a) that the commission of the offence was due to a mistake, or to reliance on information supplied to him, or to the act or default of another person, an accident, or some other cause beyond his control; and

b) that he took all reasonable precautions and exercised all due diligence to avoid the commission of such an offence by himself or any person under his control.

The courts will demand clear evidence from a supplier before accepting either of the above as a defence.

Now read the Key points from Chapter 10.

Key points from Chapter 10.

- The 1968 Trade Description Act regulates the way businesses describe their goods

- Breach of the Trade Descriptions Act is a criminal offence

- Breach of the Trade Descriptions Act is only committed by someone in the course of business

# 11

## THE CONSUMER AND
## UNSAFE GOODS

In the previous chapter we looked at the Trade Descriptions Act 1968 and how this affects the consumer. In this chapter we will look at the all important are of the consumer and unsafe goods.

Sometimes the consumer purchases a good which, when tested, turns out to be unsafe. If a contract exists between the consumer and retailer then the Sale of Goods Act s14 will give protection. If no such contract exists then the Consumer Protection Act will apply. The Consumer Protection Act 1987 also provides for criminal liability.

The Consumer Protection Act is not aimed at shoddy goods, but at unsafe goods. The Act sets out a general offence of supplying consumer goods which are not reasonably safe, provides for safety regulations to be made for products and provides for a system of notices to assist trading standards officers to enforce the Act.

Many consumer goods are controlled, or the safety of goods is controlled by detailed regulations related to the manufacture of a particular good. However, the Consumer Protection Act provides for a general safety standard. Section 19 of the Act defines what is "safe" and states:

'Safe' in relation to any goods means that there is no risk, or no risk apart from one reduced to a minimum. Therefore, goods do not have to be 100 safe. This is probably an impossibility. However, the risk of unsafe goods must be reduced to a minimum.

A person is guilty of an offence if he supplies any consumer goods which fail to comply with the general safety requirement, offers or agrees to supply any such good or exposes or possesses any such goods for supply.

Section 10 (1) and (2) are the relevant sections of the Act and section 10(2) contains a list of factors to be taken into account.

There are, as with all areas of law, recognised defences to the supply of unsafe goods. The important ones are:

a) the goods conform in a relevant respect with a European Community obligation;

b) the goods conform to any applicable safety regulations or safety standards set out by the Secretary of State for Trade and Industry for the purpose of the general safety requirement

c) that the offenders reasonably believed that the goods would not be used or consumed in the United Kingdom;

d) that the goods were supplied in the course of a business and that at the time the retailer did not know or had no reasonable grounds for believing that the goods failed to comply with the general safety requirements.;

e) that the goods were not supplied as new. The general safety requirement does not apply to second hand goods.

Penalties for contravention of the law can be up to £5,000 fine or six months in prison. However, this can vary greatly and a trader on trial for manslaughter can expect a higher sentence.

The European Community has been very active in this area and the current position is that a General Product Safety Directive has been issued to standardise the safety of food throughout Europe and was introduced onto the Statute books in.1999.

Now read the Key points from Chapter 11.

66

## Key points from Chapter 11

- If a contract exists between buyer and seller then the Sale of Goods act will apply to unsafe goods. If no such contract exists then the Consumer Protection Act 1987 will apply

- The Act sets out a general offence of supplying consumer goods which are not reasonably safe and provides for safety regulations to be made for products

- The European Community has also produced directives in this area

# 12

# FOOD SAFETY

In the previous chapter we looked at the rights of the consumer and unsafe goods. In this chapter we look at the all important are of food and health and safety.

Food poisoning is an increasing problem in our society and in the last decade there has been a massive increase in the number of reported cases. The major protection for the consumer in this area is the 1990 Food Safety Act. The aim of the Act is to control all aspects of food safety throughout the food distribution chain. Breaches of the Act result in criminal liability. There is an unlimited fine attached to breaches of the Act and also a maximum prison term of two years.

Section 7 of the 1990 Food Safety Act creates a specific offence of rendering food injurious to health with the intent that it should be sold for human consumption. The offence can be committed in several ways:

a) by adding any article or substance to the food
b) by using any article or substance as an ingredient in the preparation of food
c) abstracting any constituent from the food;
d) subjecting the food to any other process or treatment.
Section 8 of the Act also creates a number of offences and states:

"Any person who sells for human consumption or offers, exposes or advertises for sale for such consumption or has in his possession for the purpose of such sale or of preparation for such sale any food which fails to comply with food safety requirements shall be guilty of an offence"

Food can be unfit for human consumption even if it poses no health hazard. This is relevant to food which has started to incur mould growth.

The Food Safety Act also deals with food which misleads consumers. Section 14 states that anyone who sells food which is, by substance, not of the nature and quality demanded by the consumer is guilty of an offence, namely that of misleading the consumer. There are many examples here, particularly concerning meat and meat substitutes, i.e., fat instead of mince and fish. Section 15 of the Act Deals with the labelling of food and attempts to mislead by false claims.

The Act also contains many powers for food inspectors to inspect and seize food and to close down premises.

There are, as with the other areas of law, defences to breaches of the Act. One main defence is that of due diligence. However, in common with the other areas, defences have to be sound and backed up with concrete evidence.

Now read the key points from Chapter 12.

Key points from Chapter 12

- The major protection for the consumer in the are of food is the 1990 Food safety Act

- The Act contains many powers for inspectors to inspect and seize food and close down premises

# 13

# CONTROL OF PRICES

Many consumers find themselves in the position of thinking that they have a bargain and when it comes to paying for the good find that the price is higher than they thought.

Part 111 of the Consumer Protection Act 1987 controls, or regulates prices. The Act makes it a criminal offence to give consumers a misleading price indication about goods or services or accommodation. However, the Act only creates a general offence. It empowers the Secretary of State to approve a code of practice setting out guidelines for retailers as to the practice that they ought to follow. The Act does not actually require the retailer to follow the code.

The important fact is that it is only a code of practice. Misleading is defined in section 21 of the Act and covers indications about any conditions attached to a price, about future prices, price comparisons, as well as indications about the actual price the consumer will have to pay. The Act is enforced by the local Trading Standards Officers. The following guidance is given to retailers in the Code:

## Price comparisons

a) the higher price as well as the price the retailer intends to charge should always be stated. Therefore, £5 reduced to £3 is good, but sale price £6 is misleading

b) in any comparison between the present selling price and another price, the previous price as well as the new lower price should be stated.

c) the product should have been available to consumers for at least 28 consecutive days in the last six months and in the same shop where the reduced price is being offered. If not, then this should be made clear

d) general disclaimers should not be used but specific stores and prices should be referred to.

Again, this is a code of guidance and retailers do not have to follow it. However, the retail industry is attempting to be self-regulating.

## Introductory Offers
a) an introductory offer should not be described as such unless it is intended to charge a higher price later
b) an introductory offer should not be allowed to run overlong
c) future increased prices can be quoted e.g. "our price now, until next year is £250. After this period it will be £480.

## Comparison to prices related to different circumstances
The most common guidelines here are:

a) For goods in a totally different state, e.g. goods in a kit form as opposed to assembled

b) reductions for pensioners on certain days. These must be expressed in such a way that consumers are not misled and the goods or services must be available at the higher price.

## References to worth or value
Price comparisons with another trader's prices are allowed. Statements should not be made along the lines of "if you can buy for less we will refund the difference" unless the offer applies to another traders equivalent goods.

## Actual price to the consumer

The Act makes it an offence to indicate a price for goods or services which is lower than the one that actually applies. Extras such as delivery charges and postage must be clearly indicated.

## Service charges

These should be stated if they are non optional and should be incorporated in the price if possible or practicable. Extra non-optional charges can be made but these must be drawn to the customer's attention.

## Price Marking

The Price Marking Order 1991, made under the 1974 Prices Act implements two European Directives concerning prices, one in relation to food and the other in relation to non food products. This states that the selling price and, in certain cases, the unit price of goods which may be for sale by retail must be indicated in writing. Guidance is given to retailers as to where the price should be shown.

Now read the key points from Chapter 13.

## Key points from Chapter 13

- Part 111 of the Consumer Protection Act 1987 controls prices of goods

- The Act is enforced by the local Trading Standards Officer

# 14

## CONSUMER REMEDIES

There are a number of remedies available to the consumer. The Principal remedy is that through the civil courts-more specifically the small claims court, which is part of the county court. What follows is a description of the small claims procedure and of remedies available to the aggrieved consumer. Following this there will be a description of other remedies, such as the office of fair-trading.

### The Small Claims Court
The first fact to be aware of when taking a trader to court in order to obtain some sort of compensation is that it is not necessary to have either legal knowledge or use a solicitor when using the small claims procedure in the County Court.

### Commencing a claim

A person can start legal action in any court and if the case is defended the court will decide what procedure to use. If the case is a simple one, with a value of £5000 or less, the court will decide that the small claims procedure will be used and will allocate the case to the small claims track. In most cases, the court will not order that costs are paid by the losing party in a small claims case. For this reason, most people do not use a solicitor when making a small claim. It may, however, be possible to get legal help using the legal help scheme.

## Types of case dealt with in the small claims track

When the court is considering whether to allocate the case to a small claims track it will take into account a number of factors, but the main factor is the value of the case.

If the value of a case is £5000 or less it will generally be allocated to the small claims track. However, if it is a personal injury claim, it will be allocated to the small claims track only if the value of the claim for the personal injuries is not more than £1000. If the claimant is a tenant and is claiming against their landlord because repairs are needed to the premises and the cost of the work is £1000 or less, the case will be allocated to the small claims track.

## Types of claims in the small claims court

The most common types of small claims are:

- Compensation for faulty goods, for example washing machines or other goods that go wrong
- Compensation for faulty services provided, for example by builders, garages and so on
- Disputes between landlords and tenants, for examples, rent arrears, compensation for not doing repairs
- Wages owed or money in lieu of notice

If a case proves to be too complex then a judge may refer the case to another track for a full hearing, even if below the limit for that track.

## Actions before applying to court

As we saw in the previous chapter, before applying to court it is always necessary to try to solve the problem amicably, or as amicably as possible without recourse to legal action. A person who intends to commence a claim should write a 'letter before action' which should set out terms for settlement before applying to court.

For example, if a television is defective, or workmanship on a car is faulty, there is no point applying to court for compensation before contacting the garage or repair shop. Whilst this may seem obvious, there are cases where people do rush in. Always try to settle before launching court action. It will assist in the case if it does go to court.

## Which court deals with a small claim

The court action can be started in any court, but the case can be transferred. If the claim is defended and the claim is for a fixed amount, the court will automatically transfer the case to a defendant's local court (if he or she is an individual not a company). In other cases, either party can ask for the case to be transferred.

## Commencing a claim

The claimant commences a claim by filling in a claim form, obtainable from local county courts or legal stationers. They can also be obtained from the internet. The government court site is www.Courtservice.gov.uk. All forms can be obtained from this website as can a host of information on all legal topics.

The form is quite straightforward and asks for details of claimant and defendant and how much is owed. The form also asks for the particulars of the claim. The particulars set out full details of the claim. If there is not enough room on the form then a separate piece of paper can be used. The claimant has a right to spend a little more time on the particulars and can send them to the defendant separately, but no later than 14 days after the claim form.

The forms are designed to be user friendly and are accompanied by guidance notes to ensure that no mistakes are made.

The claimant may be entitled to claim interest on the claim and, if so, must give details of the interest claimed in the particulars of claim. In a personal injury claim the particulars of claim must include the claimants date of birth and brief details of the injuries. The claimant must attach a list of any past expenses and losses that they want to claim for and any expenses and losses that they may incur in the future.

## Applying for the claim form to be issued

The claimant must ensure that two copies of the claim form reach the court where court action is to commence and a copy should be kept for records. There will be a fee to pay. Currently this depends on the amount of money to be claimed. You should check with your local county court, small claims division, for the current fees.

In some cases, the fee will be waived, for example if the claimant is receiving income support, working families tax credit, disabled persons tax credit or income based job seekers allowance. If none of these benefits are received, but financial hardship would be suffered if a fee was paid, the fee may also be waived. The court will stamp the claim form and then, in most cases, serve it on the defendant. The court will give the claimant a notice of issue.

Usually the court will serve the claim form by sending it to the defendant by first class post. The claimant will be deemed to have received it on the second day of posting. If the claimant wishes to serve the claim form his or herself then a request should be made and the court will provide the form and other forms that go with it.

## If the case is not defended

If the defendant is not defending the case, then he or she may accept that they owe the money. If this is the case then he or she can pay the money directly to the claimant. If the defendant has accepted that they owe the money, but needs time to pay, they can propose an arrangement, for example that the amount owed is paid in instalments or all the money in one lump sum on a specified future date. If the claimant accepts this offer, he or she will have to return a form to the court requesting 'judgement by admission'. If the defendant does not keep to this agreement the claimant can then take enforcement action.

If the claimant does not accept this offer then he or she must give good reason and a court official will decide what a reasonable arrangement will be. The court will send both parties an order for payment. If the claimant is not happy with the order then he or she will have to write to the court giving reasons and sending a copy to the defendant. A judge will then decide what is reasonable for the defendant to pay. If the defendant does not keep to the arrangement, the claimant can take enforcement action.

## If the defendant is defending the case

If the case is to be defended, the defendant has to respond to the claim within 14 days of service (this is the second day of posting). If the particulars of claim were served after the claim form the defendant must respond within 14 days of service of particulars of claim. A defence is launched by the defendant sending back the defence form, which was sent with the claim form.

If the defendant does not send a defence back within the time period then the claimant can ask for an order to be made against him or her.

The defendant can send the defence back to the court or can send the acknowledgement of service form sent with the defence form back to court and the defence form back within 14 days of this. This helps if more time is needed.

When the defence is sent to the court the court will send an allocation questionnaire to both the claimant and the defendant. This must be returned to the court no later than the date specified in it. When the claimant returns the allocation form a fee should also be sent although this can be waived on financial grounds. The court will use the information contained within the allocation questionnaire to decide which track to allocate the case to.

When the court has decided to allocate the case to the small claims track, the claimant and defendant will be sent a notice of allocation. This form will tell the parties what they have to do to prepare for the hearing. These instructions are called 'directions'. One example of directions may be that parties are told that they should send all copies of relevant documents to court, documents that they intend to use in court in the case against the other party. These are sent at least 14 days before the case begins.

There are standard directions for a number of common cases, for example, if the claim is to do with a holiday then there will be standard directions from the courts as to the evidence needed.

## The day of the hearing

The notice of allocation will usually specify the time, day and date of hearing, where the hearing will take place and how much time has been allowed for it. If the claimant wants to attend the hearing but for some reason cannot, then a letter should be sent to the court requesting a different hearing date. A fee is payable and the court will only agree to this request if it is based on reasonable grounds.

A claimant can also ask the court to deal with a claim in his or her absence, A typical case might be where the costs and time to reach the court are disproportionate. If this is the case then a letter should reach the court at least seven days before the case.

In some cases, the court will not set a final hearing date. The following are alternatives used by the courts:

- The court could propose that the case is dealt with without a hearing. If both parties have no objections then the case can be decided on the papers only. If the parties do not reply by the date given then the court will usually take that silence as consent

- The court may hold a preliminary hearing. This could happen if the claim requires special directions which the judge wants to explain to the parties personally or where the judge feels that the claimant or defendant has no real prospect of succeeding and wants to sort out the claim as soon as possible to save everyone time and expense, or if the papers do not show any reasonable grounds for bringing the claim. A preliminary hearing could become a final hearing where the case is decided.

## Preparing a case

It is important that a case is prepared carefully – the court has to be convinced. A reasonable amount of time should be spent ensuring that all the facts are entered, all dates specified and all paperwork is available. The following points are a general guide to what preparation should be made:

- someone with low income can use the legal help scheme to cover the costs of legal advice, but not representation from a solicitor. This advice can be extremely useful and can include getting expert reports, for example on faulty goods. However, a report can only be used in court with permission of the court
- notes about the case should be set out in date order. This will help you to present your case and will make sense to a judge. All backing documentation should
- be taken to court and be presented if asked for. This documentation should be organised around the presentation, in chronological order

- damaged or faulty goods should be taken as evidence. If it is not possible to do this then photographs should be taken instead
- evidence of expenses should be taken along and any receipts kept
- all letters about the case should be taken to court
- in most cases, the claimant and defendant may be the only witnesses. If the court has agreed that other witnesses can attend, then they must attend. If a witness has difficulty getting time off work then a witness summons can be served. The courts will explain how to do this.

### The final hearing

The final hearing is usually held in public but can be held in private if the parties agree or the judge thinks that it is necessary. Hearings in the small claims track are informal and the usual rules of evidence do not apply. The judge can adopt any method of dealing with the hearing that he or she thinks fit and can also ask questions of the witnesses before anyone else. A lay representative has the right to speak on behalf of a person at a hearing but only if that party attends the hearing.

If an interpreter is needed, because English is not the first language then an experienced advisor should be consulted, or the court may be able to advise on this.

At the end of the hearing the judge will pass judgement. The judge has to give reasons for the decision that he or she has arrived at. If the claimant wins, he or she will get the court fee back as well as the sum awarded. If the claimant loses no fees will be returned. However, it is unlikely that any other costs will have to be paid.

### Appealing against a decision

A party may appeal against a judgement in the small claims track only if the court made a mistake in law or there was a serious irregularity in the proceedings. If a person wishes to appeal then a notice of appeal must be filed within 14 days. A fee is payable although this can be waived in cases of financial hardship. If you do wish to appeal a decision, it is very likely that you would need to consult a solicitor or an experienced advisor to help you.

## Enforcement of orders

If a defendant does not pay, the claimant can go back to court and enforce that order. As we have seen, there are a number of remedies, such as bailiff, attachment of earnings and garnishee order. Another fee is involved when enforcing. The court will give you full details of different remedies and fees involved.

Now read the key points from Chapter 14.

## Key points from Chapter 14

- The principal remedy for the consumer is that of the small claims court – the small claims court is a division of the county court

- There are a number of 'tracks' in the small claims court, the track used will depend on the type and amount of claim.

- It is important to try to solve a case informally before applying to court

- The county court can refer the case to a magistrates or higher court if a criminal offence has been committed

# 15

# OTHER REMEDIES

In addition to using the small claims court, there are a number of other avenue to explore when wishing to take action against a trader.

Many retailers belong to Trade Associations and that Association may give assistance to consumers. There are also codes of practice that govern various industries, such as ABTA, which governs the tourist industry.

Rather than use the court system, the consumer cannot be forced to use an arbitration scheme as opposed to the court system (Consumer Arbitration Agreements Act 1988).

Many consumers report their complaints to Local Trading Standards Departments. Detailed figures are passed on to the office of fair-trading in London. The Fair Trading Act 1973 enables the Director General of the office of Fair Trading to take action to halt practices that are harmful to consumers and to pursue individual traders whom he believes have persisted in unfair trading.

One very important avenue of complaint and subsequent action is the local authority covering an area. Trading Standards officers and Environmental Health Officers have significant power to regulate and bring action against, unscrupulous traders.

....................................

# 16

# CONSUMER LAW IN SCOTLAND

As discussed in the introduction to this book, many of the consumer laws referred to in this book apply to Scotland as well as the rest of the United Kingdom. However, there are some differences, notably in the use of the court system to obtain remedies.

Little of the Supply of Goods and services Act 1982 applies to Scotland. However, consumers have similar rights under Scottish common law.

Scottish law gives consumers five years, as opposed to six, after a purchase to take action if a problem has been discovered.

Consumers in Scotland and those who have bought items in Scotland have significantly different legal rights in the Scottish court system. For civil disputes, people take action mainly in the Sheriff Courts. Most consumer disputes are heard under a special small claims part of the 'summary cause' proceedings which, like the small claims procedure in the English, Welsh and Northern Irish county courts, is designed to be used without the need for solicitors. It has a maximum limit of £750.

It is also possible to bring an action under a normal (and more formal) 'summary cause' proceedings up to a maximum of £1500. Above this limit, consumers have to use the 'ordinary cause' proceedings in the Sheriff Court, or, if they choose, the Outer House of the Court Session.

Court proceedings in the Scottish Courts do differ considerably from the rest of the United Kingdom. Trading Standards Departments in Scotland enforce criminal consumer laws in the same way as the rest of the UK. They do not prosecute offenders themselves but investigate the facts and submit reports to the Procurator Fiscal where necessary. It is the Procurator Fiscal who decides whether or not prosecution is in the public interest. Claims for compensation for aggrieved consumers can be submitted by the Trading Standards Department in their report to the procurator Fiscal.

Scottish Criminal Law requires that most evidence is corroborated i.e. evidence is provided from two independent sources.

This is a very brief overview of the main differences between Scottish law and the rest of the UK. Separate publications deal with Scottish Consumer law in more depth.

## Sample letters of complaint
## Draft Letter: How to Complain About. . . Poor Workmanship

Dear

### {Insert Job and date}

I am writing to complain about the poor standard of workmanship I received in relation to the above job. As evidence of this I enclose a list of the problems. The work was clearly not carried out with reasonable care and skill (as required by section 13 Supply of Goods and Services Act) and, as such, amounts to a breach of contract.

Unless and until, these matters are rectified, I shall be withholding the balance of the contract price. Furthermore, if you do not put matters right within two weeks (or such other period as we may agree) I shall get another contractor to do it.

I will obtain a few quotations from reputable contractors and if the cost of the cheapest exceeds the balance of the contract price, I shall claim the extra from you by way of damages.

I will also report the matter to the Association, of which I note you are a member.

I await hearing from you.
Yours

## Draft Letter: How to Complain By. . . Withholding Payment

Dear

I am writing to notify you about why, and on what basis I am Withholding £
from the amount Owing on my account.

On {date} I entered into a contract with        for the
The    contract    price    was    £               And    I    paid    using    my
Card (see enclosed copy page from my card account).

### {Explain nature of problem (eg defective service/goods))

### {Explain why matter has not been resolved by the supplier (eg not acknowledging complaint or gone out of business))

As the cash price of the goods/service was Over £100 and as I paid using my
card, you, as the card issuer, are liable to the same extent as the supplier
(section 75 Consumer Credit Act). Consequently, as        {name of supplier)
has not satisfied my claim for breach of contract, i am legally entitled to
withhold money representing the amount of my claim from you, and you
cannot charge me interest on it.

To explain why I am withholding £      , I enclose photocopies of three
quotations I have obtained as to the cost of putting matters rights. You will
see that £   is the amount of the cheapest.

Please acknowledge receipt of this letter, and confirm you will not be
charging interest on £      withheld (unless and until the supplier actually
satisfies my claim).

I await hearing from you.
Yours

# Draft Letter: How to Complain About... Holidays

Dear _____

## {Location and Dates of Holiday}

Name in which booking was made
Hotel Name
Resort
Departure Date
Booking Reference Number

I am writing to complain about the above holiday from which I have just returned with my family. It was most disappointing.

I enclose a list of our complaints. The main one was the fact that the (accommodation/facilities) was/were not _____ as described in the brochure (see enclosed photocopy extract from the brochure). Instead the (accommodation/facilities) was/were _____

I immediately contacted your representative at the resort, but he/she was unable to resolve the matter. He/she apologised and told me to complain when I got home.

As our holiday was a package, the Package Travel Regulations 1992 apply to it. Under these regulations you are liable to compensate us for the problems we encountered and for the distress and disappointment we suffered as a result.

If this matter cannot be resolved amicably, I shall send a copy of this letter and enclosures to ABTA (of which I note you are a member). (Also, if, as I suspect, the misdescription in the brochure was made 'knowingly' or 'recklessly' by you, you will have committed a criminal offence under the Trade Descriptions Act. Accordingly, I will report it to the trading standards department of my local authority for investigation).

I await hearing from you.

Yours

## Draft Letter: How to Complain By. . .Canceling an Order

Dear _____

**(Upate/Nature of Order)**

I am writing to cancel the above order which I placed with you **{include appropriate means of distance communication eg over the telephone)**

As the contract was made at a distance, it is governed by the Distance Selling Regulations 2000. Under these regulations I have a cancellation period of seven working days from receipt of the goods.

The goods were delivered to my home yesterday, but when I unpacked them I realised that they were not appropriate for my needs. This is why I am canceling the contract. Consequently, please return the deposit I paid, and arrange to collect the goods at your earliest convenience.

Unless and until I receive written notice from you about collection and in any event, a refund of my deposit I will keep the contract goods. I will, of course, take reasonable care of them pending collection.

Under the Distance Selling Regulations, notice of cancellation which is posted is deemed effective on the date of posting. I will be posting this letter today, so please treat cancellation as effective from today's date.

I await hearing from you.

Yours

# Useful Addresses

## Advertising Standards Authority
2-16 Torrington Place
London WC1E 7HN
020 7580 5555

## Association of British Travel Agents
55-57 Newman Street
London W1P 4AH
020 7637 2444

## Association of Manufacturers of Domestic Electrical
Appliances
AMDEA House
593 Hitchin Road
Stopsley
Luton Beds LU2 7UN

## British Insurance Association
Aldermary House
Queen Street
London EC4P 4JD
020 7623 9043

## British Standards Institution

2 Park Street

London W1A 2BS

020 7629 9000

## Consumers Association

14 Buckingham Street

London WC2 6DS

020 7839 1222

## Footwear Distributors Association

Commonwealth House

1-19 New Oxford Street

London WC1A 1PA

020 7409 0955

## Insurance Ombudsman Bureau

31 Southampton Row

London WC1B 5HJ

020 7242 8613

## The Mail Order Traders Association of Great Britain

25 Castle Street

Liverpool L2 4TD

0151 227 4181

**Motor Agents Association**

73 Park Street

Bristol BS1 5PS

01272 293232


**National Association of Funeral Directors**

57 Doughty Street

London WC1N 2NE

020 7242 9388


**National Association of Retail Furnishers**

17-21 George Street

Croydon CR9 1TQ

O20 8680 8444


**National Consumer Council**

18 Queen Annes Gate

London SW1H 9AA

020 8222 9501

**National Pharmaceutical Association**

Mallinson House

40-42 St Peters Street

St Albans

Herts AL1 3NT

01727 321161

**Office of Fair Trading**

Field House

Breams Buildings

London EC4A 1PR

020 7323 4641


**Radio, electrical and Television Retailers Association**

RETRA House

57-61 Newington Causeway

London SE1 6BE

020 8 403 1463


**Scottish House Furnishers Association**

203 Pitt Street

Glasgow G2 4DB

0141 332 6381


**Scottish Motor Traders Association**

3 Palmerston Place

Edinburgh EH12 5AQ

0131 225 3643

# INDEX

Straightforward Publishing

38 Cromwell Road

London E17 9JN

0208 470 3172

For a catalogue of publications visit our web site
:www.straightforwardco.co.uk

E-mail info@straightforwardco.co.uk